MAJOR INVENTIONS THROUGH HISTORY

THE HISTORY OF
FOOD

Judith Jango-Cohen

TFCB

TWENTY-FIRST CENTURY BOOKS
Minneapolis

Dedication
To my mother, who was never too busy to prepare a good meal

Acknowledgments
The author wishes to thank Ann Kerns, editor, for the skill
and enthusiasm she brought to this project.

Twenty-First Century Books
A division of Lerner Publishing Group
241 First Avenue North
Minneapolis, MN 55401 U.S.A.

Website address: www.lernerbooks.com

Library of Congress Cataloging-in-Publication Data

Jango-Cohen, Judith.
    The history of food / by Judith Jango-Cohen.
        p.   cm. — (Major inventions through history)
    Includes bibliographical references and index.
    ISBN-13: 978-0-8225-2484-7 (lib. bdg. : alk. paper)
    ISBN-10: 0-8225-2484-8 (lib. bdg. : alk. paper)
    1. Food—Preservation—History—Juvenile literature. 2. Food—History—
Juvenile literature. I. Title. II. Series.
    TX601.J35 2006
    641.3'09—dc22   2004023022

Manufactured in the United States of America
1 2 3 4 5 6 – DP – 11 10 09 08 07 06

CONTENTS

Introduction

The Pilgrims did not have cans of spaghetti and meatballs to load onto the *Mayflower*. They packed flour, hard biscuits, dried fruit, and fish. Benjamin Franklin could not flip a frozen pizza into a microwave oven. When Franklin wanted a warm snack, he had to heat it over a fire. Frozen foods such as pizza, waffles, and fish sticks did not exist in the 1700s.

Inventions in food processing and food storage have not only changed what we eat. They have changed how we live. Once there was a world without canned, pasteurized, frozen, and genetically modified food stocked floor to ceiling in supermarkets.

What was life like then? The story is spread before you. Go on. Dig in!

CHAPTER 1

Canning

Fourteen-year-old Fernando rubs his grumbling stomach and hungers for home. Fernando is the son of Christopher Columbus. He has come along on his father's fourth voyage across the Atlantic Ocean. The trip is lasting longer than expected, and the sailors are running low on food. The food that remains is rotting.

"Even the biscuit was so full of worms," Fernando wrote. "God help me, I saw many wait until nightfall to eat . . . so as not to see the worms. Others were so used to eating them that they did not bother to pick them out."

Columbus sets sail for
the New World.
1492

A Rotten Diet

Early ocean voyages took months and sometimes years. No airplanes cruised the skies. Ships did not have huge engines to power them. Journeys over long stretches of sea were possible only on sailing ships. The ships relied on wind power, catching ocean winds in their huge sails. If a ship ran into windless weather, it could drift on the open seas for days or even weeks until it caught a wind current again.

Seafarers on these long journeys became used to spoiled food. There were no airtight, waterproof containers. There were no refrigerators. Meat was stored in barrels of salt water. The salt slowed down spoiling. But eventually the meat began to rot and stink.

Dried bread, called biscuit, became soggy on leaky ships. Beetles laid their eggs in it. Wormy weevils hatched and grew fat nibbling tunnels through the biscuits.

Cheese did not keep for long. Soon it was buzzing with flies and

GALLOPING GOURMETS

Armies in the year A.D. 450 did not have canned food. But the warriors of Attila, king of the Huns, found a clever way to preserve their meat. Galloping across Europe, the Huns placed fresh meat under their saddles. All the bouncing and bumping squeezed fluids from the meat, drying it out. The horse's sweat salted the meat, removing more moisture. Flies and beetles could not reach the meat, wedged between horse and saddle. When the warriors stopped to eat, they had a dried and salted treat.

roiling with writhing maggots. Sailors joked that the cheese was "alive" with insects. They said the cheese could walk off on its own. Rats that raided the cheese were sometimes caught and eaten by desperately hungry sailors.

With this diet, staying healthy on long sea voyages was nearly impossible. In 1497 explorer Vasco da Gama sailed from Portugal to India with 170 men. He returned two years later with a crew of only 54. A disease called scurvy had attacked the explorers. Their skin turned inky black from broken blood vessels under the skin. The explorers had trouble breathing, and their teeth fell out. Extra gum tissue grew in their mouths and began to rot. Their breath stank.

What was the cause of scurvy? Scurvy raged through the crew because there was too little vitamin C in their shipboard diet. The body needs vitamin C to keep skin, bones, and teeth healthy. Vitamin C also strengthens the walls of blood vessels. Salted meat and brick-hard biscuits did not provide enough of this nutrient. Fruits and vegetables are good sources of vitamin C. But these foods would not hold up for months at sea.

Explorers were not the only

FLOATING FARMYARD

Before canning was invented, passenger ships carried live animals. Chickens, goats, pigs, and cows provided fresh eggs, milk, and meat. But animals were not happy passengers. Some tumbled around on rocking ships and broke their legs. Others got seasick or fell overboard and drowned.

Vasco da Gama sails from
Portugal to India.
1497

British doctor James Lind
shows that citrus fruit helps
prevent scurvy.
1753

ones who suffered from dreadful diets. Soldiers on long marches and sailors fighting at sea were also ravaged by poor nutrition. In the early nineteenth century, when France and Britain were at war with each other, more soldiers and sailors died from disease than from battle.

Stopping Spoilage

Both the French and British governments realized something important. Finding a new way to preserve food (keep it from spoiling) would prevent soldiers and sailors from dying. A larger, healthier fighting force would bring a greater advantage in battle. In 1795 the French government took action. It offered a prize of 12,000 francs. The money would go to the inventor of the best-preserved food. The food had to be healthy, easily carried, and not too expensive.

In 1803 a French chef named Nicolas Appert invented a new technique for preserving food. He prepared and preserved soup, beef with gravy, beans, and peas. The French

Nicolas Appert

The French government offers a prize for food preservation.
1795

Nicolas Appert invents the first canning technique.
1803

navy stored it for three months. Then they tried it. The food was delicious—and safe to eat!

For the next few years, Appert provided the French fleet with preserved foods such as stew, milk, and juice. His preservation technique proved successful. In 1810 the French government gave Appert the prize.

How did Appert do it? The inventor filled glass bottles with food and closed the bottles with cork stoppers. He then tightened down the stoppers with wire and sealed them with a thick, waxy coating called pitch. As a final step, Appert boiled the sealed bottles in water. Food heated in the airtight bottles did not spoil.

News of Appert's discovery reached Great Britain. By 1813 the British Royal Navy was also enjoying fruit, soup, and stew. These food supplies were not bottled though. The British added their own feature to the process, sealing the prepared food in iron canisters. To keep them from rusting, the canisters were coated with tin. Unlike glass bottles, these metal containers did not break.

In 1821 an Englishman named William Underwood brought Appert's invention to the United States. Underwood set up a factory in Boston, Massachusetts, to bottle lobster and salmon. Later the factory switched from glass bottles to metal canisters. The word "can" was first used in Boston for these metal containers. Appert's preservation method became known as "canning," whether bottles or cans were used.

The French award Appert 12,000 francs for his canning technique.

1810

A London, England, factory preserves food in tin-coated iron canisters.

1813

The Demand for Cans

In 1861 the American Civil War began. Marching armies and wounded soldiers had to be fed. Canned foods provided healthy meals for thousands. Weary soldiers drew strength from canned pork and beans, oysters, stew, fruit, and milk.

Soldiers and sailors were grateful for Appert's invention. But other people were too. Canned food saved a lot of time and trouble. Before canning was invented, people had to preserve their own food. Families killed pigs and cows and salted the meat. They also dried and smoked meat over a fire. Preserved meat hung from barn rafters. Some people rubbed the meat with pepper to keep away nibbling bats. Families dried harvests of peaches, apples, beans, and corn. Milk, which soured quickly, was churned into butter or made into cheese.

Canning not only saved work and time, but it also provided a more interesting diet. Winter no longer meant just dried meat and fruit. People could choose from juicy peaches and savory stews. Canned foods could travel across oceans and continents. In the midst of grassy prairies, far from oceans, families could feast on

NO OPENERS

"Cut round the top near the outer edge with a chisel and hammer." Can openers were not invented until 1858, so early cans came with these instructions. Soldiers often ignored these directions. They opened cans with pocketknives or bayonets. Sometimes they even shot the cans open with their rifles.

William Underwood opens a canning factory in Boston, Massachusetts.
1821

Soldiers rely on canned food during the American Civil War.
1861–1865

A woman lowers a jar of peas into a canning kettle filled with boiling water. Many families canned their own food during World War II (1939–1945).

seafood. In cold regions, people could enjoy sweet pineapple from balmy lands.

For modern consumers, bottled and canned foods are a regular part of life. But they are important in emergencies too. After hurricanes or floods, canned foods quickly feed many people. Relief workers also send cans of healthful foods to people in poor nations.

An automated tin can machine is unveiled in Philadelphia, Pennsylvania.

1876

The electric can opener is introduced.

1931

Appert's preservation method was a great gift to the world. The French honored Appert as a "Benefactor of Humanity" and presented him with a gold medal. Appert had discovered that food sealed and heated in airtight containers did not spoil.

Yet he did not understand why it did not spoil. Another Frenchman, Louis Pasteur, would make that discovery.

HOT AND COLD CANS

During World War II (1939–1945), some food cans had wicks on them, like candles have. The wicks were attached to an inside tube. When soldiers lit the wick, the tube heated the food. Newer self-heating cans are easier to use. Just push a button. The button breaks a seal inside a heating cone. Water and limestone combine in the cone, releasing heat. Three minutes later, your food or drink is hot.

Self-cooling cans were harder to develop. They came along about fifty years after the self-heating kind. Astronauts were the first to use them in 1998. In one model, water evaporates inside a compartment in the can. The evaporating water draws heat from the beverage. In two to three minutes, the drink is chilled.

Carbonated soft drinks are first canned.

The U.S. canning industry booms from 5 million to 30 million cans a year.

1940

1950s

CHAPTER 2

Pasteurization

A rosy summer sun rises over New York City in 1850. Its pink light paints the roof of a shabby wooden shed. The battered barn is low and long. It has no windows.

A man lounges outside, puffing a pipe. Swatting a fly, he yawns and stretches. Then he yanks open the moldy door. Crash! Dust and cobwebs shower him from the ceiling. "Achoo!" he sneezes, wiping his nose with his hands.

The U.S. dairy industry expands as milk is shipped to cities by train.

1850s

Filthy Milk

The dairyman clomps through the dark stable and snags a metal pail. He places it under a skinny cow tied up in a stall. Kicking aside cow manure, he sets down his stool. Whirring flies burst from the flying dung. With black-nailed fingers, he squeezes milk into the pail.

Another dairyman milks a cow that is too sick to stand. The cow has to be hoisted off the floor to be milked. The men place it in a sling. Then they raise the sling with ropes.

A woman milks the family cow in the 1800s.

British doctor John Snow links germs to
an outbreak of cholera in London.

1854

When the men are done milking, they pour the milk into large metal cans. The milk seller's horse-drawn wagon hauls the cans through the city. A young woman stands waiting with an empty pitcher. As the wagon slows, a boy throws a ball. It bounces onto the wagon and hits the top of a milk can. The ball knocks off the lid and plops into the milk. Grumbling, the milk seller fishes out the floating ball. Then he turns to fill the woman's pitcher.

Learning about Germs

In the nineteenth century, people often got sick or died from drinking milk. Usually, they did not realize that the milk had made them sick. How could they? People did not know about germs. They did not know that germs burst out with a sneeze. They were unaware of germs lurking under filthy fingernails. People did not understand that sick cows spread germs through their milk. The cause of disease was a mystery.

The mystery of disease was soon solved by a French scientist named Louis Pasteur. In 1857 Pasteur was investigating batches of beet juice that manufacturers

Mysterious Germs

The bubonic plague, or "Black Death," killed millions of Europeans in the mid-1300s. Since germs were unheard of at the time, French scientists blamed the planets. They claimed that Mars, Jupiter, and Saturn had lined up together, causing the plague. In fact, the plague was caused by bacteria carried by flea-infested rats.

Louis Pasteur begins
studying how food spoils.
1857

were turning into alcohol. The process is similar to the way that grape juice is made into wine. The alcohol they produced was used to make paint, perfume, and vinegar. But instead of becoming alcohol, the beet juice often turned sour. Many distillers were losing money.

Pasteur took drops of the spoiled beet juice and inspected them under the microscope. He discovered that there, in the beet juice, were tiny living creatures! Pasteur then proved that these microbes (or germs) were causing the beet juice to spoil.

The Protection of Pasteurization

Pasteur next experimented with wine that had gone sour. He discovered that the ruined wine was also infected with germs. He tried

Pasteur investigates
wine spoilage.
1864

DISEASES AT THE DAIRY

Before pasteurization was invented, diseased cows often spread sickness to people. One disease that especially affected children was bovine (cattle) tuberculosis. Symptoms included fever, stomach pains, and weight loss. Sometimes the disease infected the spine, causing the bones to become deformed. Children who had the disease wore stiff frames to keep their spines straight. Cows can still contract bovine tuberculosis. But pasteurization has greatly reduced the risk of the disease being spread to humans through milk.

treating the wine with chemicals to kill the germs. But when he looked through the microscope, he saw that the microbes were still alive. Through more experiments, Pasteur discovered that heating closed bottles of newly made wine to 122–140°F (50–60°C) destroyed these harmful microbes. Since the bottles were closed, no new microbes could infect and spoil the wine. Pasteur's discovery finally explained that Appert's canning method had successfully preserved food by killing microbes.

Like Appert, Pasteur tried out his experiment with the French navy. One ship took five hundred bottles of wine. Half had been heated, and half had not. After ten months, only the heated wine remained unspoiled.

Pasteur's heating process became known as pasteurization. After the wine experiments, pasteurization was used on other liquids, such as vinegar, cider, beer, fruit juice, and milk. The process killed microbes that kept these products from spoiling. But it was also

Testing of U.S. dairy cattle for tuberculosis begins.
1890

Chicago, Illinois, becomes the first U.S. city to outlaw the sale of unpasteurized milk.
1908

discovered that pasteurization killed germs that cause disease. Pasteurization was especially effective in treating milk for diseases that passed from cows to humans.

The need for pasteurizing milk was not accepted at first. Many people found it hard to believe that microbes could cause disease. How could tiny, invisible creatures kill beings as big as humans? Even some doctors and scientists did not accept this idea.

A Safe Supply

Today people understand that germs spread disease. Dairies must follow strict food safety rules. Inspectors make sure workers have clean hands, fingernails, and clothes. Workers are not allowed to smoke tobacco inside the dairy. The dairy must be well lit so dirt is easily visible. Bathrooms may not open into workrooms where milk is present. The dairy should be free of rodents and insects. Milk containers must be sealed with caps that cover the pouring spout.

MIGHTY MICROBES

Do you wish someone could invent a way to get rid of all microbes? That would actually be disastrous. Not all microbes are harmful germs. We need some microbes to survive. For example, microbes produce about half of the world's oxygen. Others turn milk into yogurt and cause bread to rise. Some microbes in your stomach break down the food you eat. Otherwise you couldn't digest it. Microbes also break down garbage, dead plants, and dead animals. Imagine if everything that lived never decayed?

Ninety-eight percent of milk sold in major U.S. cities is pasteurized.

1936

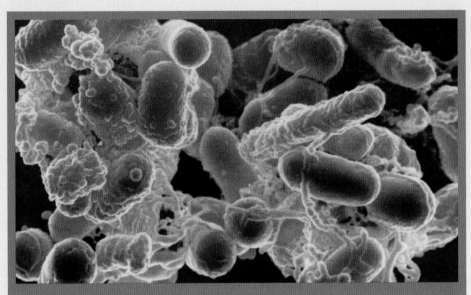

The *E. coli* bacteria grow rapidly in unpasteurized milk and undercooked meat. Eating food infected with *E. coli* can cause severe stomach cramps and diarrhea.

Laws require that only properly pasteurized milk is sold. Heating times and temperatures must be followed exactly. These procedures ensure that milk is clean and pasteurized when you buy it.

But once the container is opened, microbes can get in. Fortunately, we have found a "cool" way of slowing these microbes down. It's called refrigeration. Read on!

Labeling milk cartons with
nutrition information begins.
1974

CHAPTER 3

Refrigeration

One warm morning in 1933, two girls race down a steep street. As they run, they roll rubber tires with wooden sticks. One girl's tire topples over. The other girl reaches the bottom, panting and sweaty. Then a rumbling on the road makes the girls look up. The ice truck!

Abandoning their tires, they dash over to the truck. The iceman yanks open the truck's big doors and motions for the children to move back. Raising his pointy ice pick, he chips sparkling slivers off the frigid block. The iceman hands each child a glossy chip as a cool treat. Then he lifts the carved-out ice block with metal tongs and throws it over his shoulder. A rubber pad protects his back from the chilly chunk.

A woman holds her door open as the iceman enters. He drops the block into the top of her icebox. It will chill the food stored on the shelves below.

Cool Food

People have long known that cold temperatures preserve food. Ancient people kept food in cool caverns and deep wells. The Chinese preserved food with ice gathered from mountains and frozen streams. They stored the ice in great underground pits. At a Chinese palace in the second century A.D., ninety-four servants worked as icemen.

By the late eighteenth century, icehouses were common in the United States. Icehouses were often underground. The soil above insulated the ice, slowing its melting. Thomas Jefferson,

MICROBES AND MAMMOTHS

What does cold have to do with preserving food? Cold temperatures slow down food-spoiling microbes. Frosty temperatures "freeze" the activity of microbes—sometimes for thousands of years. In the early 1800s, a woolly mammoth was found preserved in ice. A professor defrosted, cooked, and served the mammoth to his dinner guests. After dinner he told them that they had just eaten one-thousand-year-old meat.

Icehouses are common in colonial America.

1700s

the third U.S. president, had an icehouse built on his Virginia estate, Monticello. Monticello's icehouse held sixty-two wagonloads of ice. It preserved meat and butter and kept wine chilled. Jefferson also used the ice to make ice cream. Smaller farms needed icehouses too. Farmers cut the ice from rivers or ponds with axes and saws. They hauled the ice to icehouses on sleds or wagons. Thick blankets of straw or sawdust protected the frozen stacks. Even so, half the ice often melted.

> ## WINDOW CHILLS
> In winter many Americans stopped buying ice for the icebox. They put their food outside on the windowsill instead.

A Big Business

During the 1800s, selling ice became a major business. In 1806 ice from Boston was shipped to the island of Martinique in the Caribbean Sea. By 1856 ice from the United States traveled to seaports in China, the Philippines, and Australia. Most American kitchens had iceboxes by the 1860s. Hotels, restaurants, butchers, and fish sellers all relied on ice to keep food fresh.

By the end of the 1800s, railroads crisscrossed the United States. Train boxcars cooled with ice could carry vegetables, fruit, meat, and milk. Farmers earned more money. And Americans enjoyed a wider selection of fresh foods.

British inventor Michael Faraday uses liquified ammonia in a refrigeration experiment.
1824

Workers cut ice chunks from Lake Calumet in Chicago, Illinois. Chicago's cold winters ensured a steady supply of ice.

But steady supplies of ice were not reliable. Warm winters caused ice shortages. Hot regions did not have ice at all. Ships and trains could carry ice to these hot regions, but transportation costs were high. This made the ice expensive for customers.

Creating Cold

Discoveries in the 1800s rescued people from dependence on natural ice. Scientists began experimenting with machines that produced cool air. They invented the first refrigerators and freezers.

Warm winters in the United States cause severe ice shortages.
1889–1890

These scientists had learned that when liquids evaporate (turn into gases), they draw heat away from their surroundings. For example, heated water boils away into a gas called water vapor.

Scientists conducted experiments with different liquids called refrigerants. Refrigerants are liquids that evaporate in refrigerators. As refrigerants evaporate, they take heat away from the inside of the refrigerator. This makes refrigerators and freezers cold.

Early refrigerating machines were not practical for home use. They were complicated to operate and were run by big, thumping steam engines. The refrigerants, such as ammonia and sulfur dioxide, were in a separate compartment from the food storage area. But they still gave off a revolting smell. They were also poisonous. Sometimes refrigerants leaked out and killed people. For all these reasons, refrigerators were not used in homes in the 1800s.

The Refrigeration Business

Although early refrigerators could not be used in home kitchens, meat producers and butchers quickly invested in the new devices. Ships outfitted with freezers carried cargoes of meat from South America and Australia to Europe. Refrigerators and freezers were set up in meatpacking plants. Refrigerated warehouses stored meat until it was sold to markets. With refrigeration, less meat was wasted by spoilage, so sellers could reduce the price. The lower cost meant that more people could buy meat for everyday meals.

Commercial refrigeration is used in industry, plant nurseries, clothes storage, and hospitals.

1900s

In the late nineteenth century, refrigerating machines were also used to make ice. Factory-made ice replaced natural ice in homes, stores, and restaurants. Clean ice was now available in any weather and in every climate.

Although ships were equipped with refrigerating machines, lightweight and economical refrigeration had not yet been invented for trains. Train boxcars still cooled their cargoes with ice. Ice factories sprang up near railways, allowing boxcars to carry food across the country. If ice melted along the way, it could be easily replaced.

Foods arrived on trains and ships from distant states and faraway nations. By the late 1920s, New Yorkers could buy fruits and vegetables from about nineteen different countries. Shoppers in London, England, were buying California oranges. Bananas from the Caribbean traveled as far north as Canada.

Kitchen Refrigerators

Refrigeration finally reached people's homes in the early 1900s, when problems with large engines and poisonous refrigerants were solved. By the 1930s, sleek refrigerators were being installed in home kitchens. The refrigerators had automatic controls, small electrical motors, and a nonpoisonous refrigerant. Refrigerator companies proclaimed the wonders of their product.

"Leave for the weekend without worrying about melting ice or spoiled food."

Two thousand commercial ice plants operate in the United States.

1909

General Electric unveils its home refrigerator unit in Fort Wayne, Indiana.

1911

A woman takes eggs from her kitchen refrigerator. By the 1930s, steel and porcelain refrigerators had replaced wooden iceboxes in many American homes.

"No more icemen tracking dirt into your home."

In the 1930s, Americans began buying millions of refrigerators. Later, refrigerators came with a freezer section. Instead of buying small amounts of food every day, shoppers could buy a whole week's worth of food in one trip and safely store it at home.

Frosted Foods

Freezers led to the development of a new type of food. This food was different because it was not fresh or canned. It was frozen.

The process of fast-freezing food is developed.

1923

Clarence Birdseye experiments with chopped carrots at his factory in the 1930s.

Clarence Birdseye, an inventor born in Brooklyn, New York, invented a machine that could quick-freeze fish, meats, fruits, and vegetables. Because the food was frozen quickly, it did not develop big ice crystals that ruined its flavor. When the food thawed out, it still tasted good.

Birds Eye "Frosted Foods" first went on sale in the United States on March 6, 1930. Advertisements told customers, "You can buy them ready to cook or eat! No work on your part. You will see meat, fish, oysters . . . even June peas and rich, red raspberries. Be one of the first persons in the world to try these foods!"

Clarence Birdseye
begins selling his
Frosted Foods.

Americans buy more
than one million
refrigerators.

1930   **1931**

Refrigerated Trucks and Trains

Modern shoppers regularly stock up on frozen pizza, pancakes, fish sticks, and pies. But frozen food did not catch on right away in the 1930s. People liked it, but many stores could not get it delivered. Unlike ships, which had refrigerators, trucks and trains were still chilling their cargo with ice. Ice worked fine for fruits and vegetables. But ice could not keep frozen food cold enough.

In 1939 Frederick McKinley Jones supplied the solution. Jones invented a refrigerating unit that could withstand the jostling of trucks. It could be adjusted to chill or freeze food. Nine years later, Jones designed a system for refrigerating train boxcars. By the 1950s, frozen foods were zipping around the country.

A young shopper helps her mother pick out Birds Eye frozen vegetables in the 1940s.

MINUTES IN THE MICROWAVE

When frozen food first came out, people heated it in regular ovens. Heating time was often thirty minutes to an hour. Microwaves, which can heat food in minutes, made frozen food even more convenient and popular. The first home microwave oven was introduced in 1955. It was the size of a refrigerator.

An early Birds Eye advertisement made a prediction. Frozen foods would create a new kind of store. It would not be a grocery store or a butcher shop or a fish market. It would be one store where all kinds of foods could be found. It would be a "super" market.

More than 90 percent of U.S. homes have refrigerators.

1950

Microwave ovens cook frozen food in minutes.

1955

MARKET.

CHAPTER 4

Supermarkets

On a fall day in 1900, a pigtailed girl carrying an empty pitcher enters a grocery store. The bell on the door clatters, rousing a fluffy cat. Passing crates of apples, the girl breathes in their sweet scent. She peers into a barrel of plump sour pickles. At the counter, the girl hands the pitcher to the grocer. She pulls a list from her pocket and hands him that too.

The storekeeper reaches into the cookie barrel and gives the girl a treat. Then he glances down the girl's list: milk, five pounds

In the early 1900s, most grocery stores were full-service. A store clerk took a customer's order, got the items from shelves and bins, and had the groceries delivered to the customer's house.

(2.3 kilograms) of sugar, one pound (.5 kg) of crackers, three pounds (1.4 kg) of coffee, and two pounds (.9 kg) of cheese. Ladling milk from a tin can into the girl's pitcher, the grocer tells the girl he'll deliver the rest of the groceries to her house. As the girl leaves, the cat swirls around her legs, hoping a bit of milk will spill.

With a stubby pencil, the grocer adds up the price of the order. The family will pay him next week, when their paycheck comes. The grocer wraps up the ordered groceries in paper and

Most grocery stores have clerks
who fill customers' orders.

1900s

string. After the groceries are packaged, the store's delivery clerk will load them into his bicycle basket and deliver them to the customer.

The First Self-Service

A young man named Clarence Saunders worked in a grocery store like this in Memphis, Tennessee. But Saunders wasn't happy with the way the store did business. He thought that selling food took too long. Groceries had to be weighed and wrapped. Some customers took up time bargaining about the price. Delivering food took hours too. Keeping track of how much money people owed was another chore.

Saunders believed he could invent a quicker way to sell groceries. He noticed that some food companies had stopped packing goods in huge barrels and crates. They had begun to package food in small bags and cartons. Saunders realized that if he sold only packaged foods, he wouldn't have to scoop and measure. Customers could serve themselves. Self-service would speed things up. And he could hire fewer workers, saving money.

Saunders realized that he could save time and money in other ways too. Customers could carry out their own food. They could pay in cash as they bought it. This system came to be called "cash-and-carry." Cash-and-carry and self-service meant lower costs for Saunders and better prices for his customers.

In 1916 Saunders put these ideas to the test. He opened the first self-service grocery store in Memphis, Tennessee. Saunders called it the Piggly Wiggly. The store was laid out in aisles with shelves full of packaged and priced items. Customers followed a one-way path until they reached the cashier at the exit. The route took customers through every aisle of the store. Walking past all the food made customers buy more. The low prices did too.

By 1918 Piggly Wiggly self-service grocery stores were a hit with shoppers.

Clarence Saunders opens the
first self-service grocery store.

1916

"Super" Markets

Saunders's shopping invention was a hit with customers. Piggly Wiggly markets opened nationwide. Thousands of other grocery stores throughout the United States switched to self-service, selling canned and packaged foods. In the 1930s, these stores added fresh fruits, vegetables, and bakery items. They also installed refrigerated cases stocked with packaged meat and dairy products. The small self-service market had turned into a "super" market. One-stop shopping was here! Neighborhood butcher shops, fruit stands, and door-to-door milkmen began to disappear.

Modern supermarket shoppers weave their way through dizzying displays of food. Customers are not herded onto a set path as in the original Piggly Wiggly. But supermarkets have other ways of tempting customers to fill their carts. Bakeries are often near the

BASKETS ON WHEELS

Imagine if supermarkets only had handbaskets for carrying food. The first supermarkets did.

Shoppers would fill a basket or maybe two. Then they would have to head for the checkout because they couldn't carry any more. In 1937 Sylvan Goldman, a grocer, figured out how his customers could buy more. He invented large baskets on wheels, called shopping carts. At first, most customers did not want to try these weird-looking baskets. So Goldman hired people to use the carts, pretending to be customers. When shoppers saw other people pushing the carts, they tried them too. Today a cart is the first item most customers grab.

The first supermarket, King Cullen, opens in Queens, New York.

1930

BAR CODES

Bar codes are a familiar sight in modern supermarkets. The little labels of black bars and numbers were first printed on food packages in the 1970s. The labels are coded with price information for computer cash registers. Before bar codes, stock clerks had to print out and paste price tags on every can or package in the store. Check-out clerks memorized the cost of items that didn't get price tags, such as fresh vegetables. At checkout, a clerk punched in the price of every purchase on the cash register. But with bar codes, a check-out clerk simply passes an item's label over a scanner. Inside the scanner, a beam of light called a laser reads the bar code's information and sends it to the computer cash register. The name of the item, its price, and its manufacturer all print out on the cash register's receipt.

entrance. The sweet smells lure shoppers toward cupcakes and cookies. Food for small children is usually on low shelves, where they can grab it. Check-out lines are set up so that waiting customers face displays of candy bars, chilled drinks, and gum.

Some supermarkets have begun offering customers a virtual shopping experience. Customers can visit a supermarket's website on the Internet. The website includes photographs of food items, prices, brand names, and package size or weight. As a customer clicks on items, an electronic shopping cart fills up. After electronic checkout, the items are delivered to the customer's house (in a real truck, of course).

Thousands of different foods roll through supermarket checkouts. Most of the foods have been

Bar codes are printed on food packages.

1970s

A grocery store clerk runs an item's bar code over the scanner. With bar codes, clerks do not have to type in all prices or remember sales.

changed, or modified, in some way. There is pasteurized milk and cheese, frozen pizza and peas, and cans of meat and beans. But some foods have been modified in another way. Since the mid-1990s, genetically modified foods have moved into your market.

UNRULY CUSTOMERS

Professor John Trinkaus, from Baruch College in New York, studies shoppers in supermarkets. He discovered that customers do not always follow the rules. Ninety percent of people pick up pastries or rolls with their hands instead of tongs. Eighty-five percent take too many items through the express line.

Researchers predict that Internet grocery sales will almost double every year through 2008.

2004

CHAPTER 5

Genetically Modified Foods

In 1964 a scientist climbs through the dry highlands of southern Mexico. He reaches a cave snuggled against a cliff. Thousands of years ago, people may have found shelter here. For six days, the scientist digs through a squared-off patch of ground. He gently unearths corncobs the size of a thumbnail. They are about five thousand years old. How did these tiny corncobs become the colossal corn we eat in the twenty-first century?

Human Impact

Agricultural history began when people stopped gathering wild crops like corn and started planting it themselves. Collecting their crop, early farmers noticed that some corn plants were larger than others. Kernels from these larger cobs produced other large plants. Somehow, parent plants were passing the trait, or quality, of large size to their offspring. By selecting only the largest seeds from each crop, farmers developed small cobs into supersized ones.

Breeding plants or animals for certain traits is called artificial selection. In artificial selection, people choose which plants and animals will reproduce. They select the plants and animals for good or useful traits. For example, farmers choose fast-growing wheat or breeders select sheep with thick wool.

All of the foods we grow and the animals we raise are products of artificial selection. Newer types of tomatoes are monsters compared to their grape-sized ancestors. Pigs are much heftier than they were thousands of years ago. Modern dairy cows give significantly more milk. Some modern

A New Fruit

Scientists breed plants to create sweeter, bigger, or hardier varieties. But scientists have also created new plants through breeding. In 1931, for example, the U.S. Department of Agriculture combined a tangerine and a grapefruit to create the Minneola. The Minneola looks like an orange with a bump on one end.

breeds of chicken lay about three hundred eggs per year. Their wild relatives lay a yearly clutch (bunch) of only about one dozen eggs.

Discovering DNA

For thousands of years, people had no idea exactly how traits passed from parent to offspring. In 1865 an Austrian monk named Gregor Mendel uncovered part of the mystery. Mendel experimented with 28,000 pea plants in his monastery garden. His experiments convinced him that parents pass traits to their offspring in packets. These packets became known as genes. In the next century, scientists discovered that genes are composed of a chemical called DNA.

Scientists experimented with DNA in the 1960s and 1970s. They learned how to snip out the DNA for a selected gene. They also learned how to reattach it. In 1973 scientists Herbert Boyer and Stanley Cohen did something unheard of. They removed a gene from an African clawed toad and placed it into bacteria. Bacteria are microscopic organisms, only visible through a microscope.

THE FULL NAME

The material that makes up genes is abbreviated as DNA. This is because its full name is rather long. DNA stands for deoxyribonucleic acid.

With Boyer and Cohen's work, scientists had found a way to remove a particular gene and place it into another organism. Bacteria genes could become part of plants and animals. Animal

Boyer and Cohen
experiment with
interchanging genes.
1973

Minneolas ripen in the sun.

and plant genes could be inter-
changed. Scientists could even
modify, or change, a chosen gene.
Organisms whose genes have been
changed in any of these ways are re-
ferred to as genetically modified
(GM).

The Flavr Savr

The first GM fruit reached U.S. su-
permarkets in 1994. The product is called the Flavr Savr tomato.
The Flavr Savr does not get as soft as regular tomatoes while ripen-
ing. Regular tomatoes have to be picked when they are green and
fairly hard, so they are not bruised by picking machines. Flavr
Savrs also do not rot before reaching the food store. Flavr Savrs,

The Flavr Savr tomato is
sold in U.S. supermarkets.

1994

which stayed firm for three weeks, could be left to ripen on the vine. This gave them better flavor while still preventing rot during transportation.

To create the Flavr Savr, scientists modified one of the tomato's own genes. They took out the gene that causes the tomato to soften as it ripens. Then they reattached the gene backward. The gene did not work well in its reversed position, so it slowed the softening process.

A scientist inspects a plant in a greenhouse.

Boosting Food Supplies

Genetic modifications are often designed to increase the world's food supply. Crops have been altered to grow in soil that is normally too dry or too salty. Countries can grow food in more regions than they could before. Bananas have been developed to resist disease. Corn, soybeans, and potatoes have been modified to poison insects that attack them. They have been given a bacteria gene that makes an insect poison. The poison, or pesticide, is deadly to insects but does not harm humans. More crops survive when they are armed with this gene, and farmers are able to use less pesticide, which helps protect the environment.

Animals have been genetically modified to speed up food production. For example, salmon that receive flounder genes grow faster. They reach the size of three-year-old salmon in sixteen to eighteen months. These speedy-growing salmon are also lower in fat.

A Healthier Harvest

Creating healthier food is another goal of genetic modification. In Asia many poor people live mainly on rice. This diet lacks vitamin A—a deadly problem. Without enough vitamin A, a person may go blind or even die. As a solution, scientists created golden rice. Golden rice contains genes from daffodils and bacteria. With these genes, rice produces a yellow nutrient called beta-carotene. Our bodies turn beta-carotene into vitamin A.

Golden rice is created.
1999

Questions and Concerns

Some people believe that GM food will help decrease hunger and disease. But others see GM food as a dangerous creation—a Frankenfood. They have named this food after Dr. Frankenstein, a fictional scientist who accidentally invents a monster. These critics point out that all of nature is connected in a complex food web. No plant or animal is isolated. They fear that releasing GM foods into the food web could be disastrous.

Opponents of GM food also worry about the health of people. Scientists have not tested the long-term effects of many GM foods. Will years of eating this food cause unexpected problems?

These questions remain unanswered, as GM foods crowd U.S. supermarkets. As much as two-thirds of U.S. supermarket foods may have GM ingredients. You cannot tell which ones though. Canada and the United States do not require GM foods to be labeled. Genetically modified corn may be found in cereal, corn chips, popcorn, corn oil, and soft drinks that contain corn syrup. Ingredients made from GM soybeans are added to chocolate bars, ice cream, crackers, soy sauce, and soup.

THE MATCH GAME

Matching each gene to the trait it codes for can be complicated. In 2001 researchers determined that rice has fifty thousand genes.

One-fourth of U.S. cropland
is used for GM foods.

2000

Superfood or Frankenfood?

To some people, genetically modified food is a great invention. But GM food may remind others of the apple that Eve ate. Some say it brings wonderful things. Others worry that it will bring catastrophe.

There are always those who fear change or are suspicious of new inventions. Some people were afraid of pasteurized milk. They did not want to drink the dead bacteria killed by heating.

But fear of new inventions has sometimes been justified. People did not understand, at first, how canning preserved food. They did not realize that heating killed bacteria. Sometimes very large cans were not heated long enough. Bacteria in the center of the cans were not killed. People who ate this food died. Canned food became truly safe only when Pasteur discovered how to destroy disease-causing germs.

In the 1930s, people thought they had found a safe refrigerant, called Freon. If it leaked out, it did not poison people as sulfur dioxide had. But in the 1980s, scientists discovered that Freon was harming the environment. It was destroying a part of the atmosphere called the ozone layer. Ozone shields the earth from sunrays that cause sunburn and skin cancer. Now Freon is banned.

What will the future of genetically modified food be? Superfood or Frankenfood? We will have to wait and see.

Almost 150 million acres
(60.7 million hectares) of GM
crops are grown worldwide.

2003

Epilogue

Inventions have revolutionized how and what we eat. They have provided safe, healthy food and convenient ways to buy and store it. But what's next in the field of food inventions?

Research continues on the possible benefits of GM food. Before the development of GM food, heavy doses of pesticides were necessary to keep crops safe. But the chemicals in pesticides are poisonous. Some of the poison gets into the soil and into natural water supplies. Some of it also lingers on our food. Farmers growing GM crops can greatly reduce the use of pesticides because GM crops are more resistant to plant disease and insects.

Researchers also continue to tailor GM food for greater health benefits. More nutritious and less fattening food is being designed. It is even being modified to include nutritional agents that fight cancer, heart disease, and allergies. Scientists are engineering GM foods to deliver vaccines against deadly diseases such as rabies, AIDS, and hepatitis B. These foods could be grown in developing nations where vaccines are expensive and difficult to deliver.

In addition to health and nutrition, new food technology focuses on convenience. Bar codes, first used to make checkout speedy and accurate, are being loaded with even more information. "Smart" appliances will come with sensors for reading this information. For example, a bar code on a frozen dinner may contain cooking instructions. Pass the bar code over a microwave oven's sensor, and the cooking time and power level will be automatically set. A bar code on a box of rice may contain recipe suggestions. Pass the bar code over a sensor on a kitchen counter, and recipes will be projected on the wall.

At the supermarket, a smart shopping cart may assist you with your shopping. These carts will come equipped with a computer screen and a scanner. The screen will alert you to sales. As you head down the candy aisle, it may inform you that Gooey Chews are half price. If you swipe your store card in the scanner, a history of all your purchases becomes available. Using this information, the cart may beep out a warning that you haven't bought dog food in two weeks.

Some people are worried about the loss of privacy with computers that track all their purchases. But stores are betting that convenience will overcome their customers' concerns.

1753 British doctor James Lind shows that citrus fruit helps prevent scurvy.

1803 Nicolas Appert invents the first canning technique.

1813 A London, England, factory preserves food in tin-coated iron canisters.

1821 William Underwood opens a canning factory in Boston, Massachusetts.

1824 British inventor Michael Faraday uses liquefied ammonia in a refrigeration experiment.

1850s The U.S. dairy industry expands as milk is shipped to cities by train.

1854 British doctor John Snow links germs to an outbreak of cholera in London.

1857 French scientist Louis Pasteur begins studying how food spoils.

1858 John Mason files a patent for his home canning jars. Ezra Warner invents the first can opener.

1864 Pasteur investigates wine spoilage.

1876 An automated tin can machine is unveiled in Philadelphia, Pennsylvania.

1889–1890 Warm winters in the United States cause severe ice shortages.

1890 Testing of U.S. dairy cattle for tuberculosis begins.

1908 Chicago, Illinois, becomes the first U.S. city to outlaw the sale of unpasteurized milk.

1909 Two thousand commercial ice plants operate in the United States.

1911 General Electric unveils its home refrigerator unit in Fort Wayne, Indiana.

1916 Clarence Saunders opens the first self-service grocery store.

1930 Clarence Birdseye begins selling his Frosted Foods. The first supermarket, King Cullen, opens in Queens, New York.

1931 One million refrigerators are sold in the United States. The electric can opener is introduced. Scientists create a new fruit, the Minneola.

1936 Ninety-eight percent of milk sold in major U.S. cities is pasteurized.

1939 Frederick McKinley Jones invents a truck refrigeration unit.

1940 Carbonated soft drinks are first canned.

1948 Jones invents a boxcar refrigeration system.

1950s The U.S. canning industry booms from 5 million to 30 million cans a year.

1950 More than 90 percent of U.S. homes have refrigerators.

1957 Aluminum is first used in making food cans.

1970s Bar codes are printed on food packages.

1973 Boyer and Cohen experiment with interchanging genes.

1974 Labeling milk cartons with nutrition information begins.

1994 The Flavr Savr tomato is sold in U.S. supermarkets.

2000 One-fourth of U.S. cropland is used for GM foods.

2003 Almost 150 million acres (60.7 million hectares) of GM crops are grown worldwide.

2004 Genes from GM crops have spread to two-thirds of the traditional crops grown in the United States.

2005 The Food Network, a television network devoted to cooking and modern food history, reaches 80 million U.S. households and four million website users.

GLOSSARY

bar codes: labels of bars and numbers encoded with information. Bar codes were first used on food packages in the 1970s.

canning: a way of preserving food by heating and sealing it in clean jars or cans

dairy: a building or group of buildings where milk is processed. Dairy operations can include milking cows, storing milk, and making cheese and butter.

Frankenfood: a term used by some people who argue against genetically modified food. The term compares genetically modifying food to creating a Frankenstein monster.

frozen food: food that is packaged and quickly frozen in very low temperatures

genetically modified (GM): something that has had its genes changed to produce a certain effect. Food is genetically modified to make it larger, more nutritious, or better able to resist diseases.

icebox: a wooden cabinet that includes a space for a block of ice. Before refrigerators were invented, iceboxes were used to keep food fresh.

microbes: germs, or living creatures too small to be seen without a microscope. Microbes can cause food to spoil.

nutrition: the study the necessary vitamins and minerals we get from food

pasteurization: a process of heating food and liquids to an exact temperature to kill germs. Pasteurization makes foods safe and keeps them from spoiling in their containers.

preserve: to keep something, such as food, from rotting

refrigerants: certain liquids used to make refrigerators cold. As refrigerants evaporate (turn into vapors or fumes), they draw heat out of the refrigerator.

self-service: a business where customers help themselves, rather than being waited on by an employee. In self-service grocery stores, customers choose and carry their own items.

supermarket: a store that sells many different foods and other household items

tuberculosis: an infectious disease that causes fever, stomach pain, and spinal deformities. Before milk pasteurization was common, tuberculosis often spread from cows to people.

SELECTED BIBLIOGRAPHY

Bowlby, Rachel. *Carried Away: The Invention of Modern Shopping.* New York: Columbia University Press, 2001.

Elkort, Martin. *The Secret Life of Food: A Feast of Food and Drink History, Folklore, and Fact.* Los Angeles: Jeremy P. Tarcher, 1991.

Hart, Kathleen. *Eating in the Dark: America's Experiment with Genetically Engineered Food.* New York: Pantheon Books, 2002.

Jones, Joseph. *American Ice Boxes.* Humble, TX: Jobeco Books, 1981.

Pringle, Peter. *Food, Inc.: Mendel to Monsanto—The Promises and Perils of the Biotech Harvest.* New York: Simon & Schuster, 2003.

Reynolds, Moira Davidson. *How Pasteur Changed History.* Bradenton, FL: McGuinn & McGuire Publishing, 1994.

Robertson, Una. *The Illustrated History of the Housewife, 1650–1950.* New York: St. Martin's Press, 1997.

Shephard, Sue. *Pickled, Potted, and Canned.* New York: Simon & Schuster, 2000.

Trager, James. *The Food Chronology.* New York: Henry Holt, 1995.

FURTHER READING AND WEBSITES

Dairysville

http://www.creamland.com/mteamdairysville.html

The story of milk from "cow to carton" is cleverly presented with in-depth information, diagrams, student fact sheets, and projects.

Ford, Barbara. *Keeping Things Cool.* New York: Walker and Company, 1986.
This book presents the history and science of cooling, from Roman snow-packed cellars to ice-making refrigerators.

Fridell, Ron. *Genetic Engineering.* Minneapolis: Lerner Publications Company, 2005.
Fridell explains the latest developments in the science of genetic engineering.

Giblin, James Cross. *Milk: The Fight for Purity.* New York: Thomas Y. Crowell, 1986.
Giblin's unique book provides a broad history of this basic beverage, but it also brims with intriguing tidbits.

How Refrigerators Work
http://home.howstuffworks.com/refrigerator.htm
Visitors to this site will discover how the refrigerator "performs its magic." They will also learn about cold packs, electronic coolers, and the propane refrigerators in recreational vehicles.

Infection Detection Protection
http://www.amnh.org/nationalcenter/infection/index.html
This American Museum of Natural History site guides young people through topics such as the causes, spread, and prevention of infection. It features lively writing, colorful graphics, and microscopic photographs.

Inventions and Inventors: Farming, Food, and Biotechnology. Vol. 4. Danbury, CT: Grolier Educational, 2000.
This attractive volume presents the science of food with sidebars, charts, and clear, child-friendly language.

Key Ingredients: America by Food
http://www.keyingredients.org/default.asp
This online educational companion to the Smithsonian Institution's traveling exhibition takes you through five hundred years of growing, preparing, and serving foods.

Kowalski, Kathiann. *The Debate over Genetically Engineered Food*. Berkeley Heights, NJ: Enslow Publishers, 2002.
Beautifully written and carefully researched, this book is a great introduction for young readers and adults alike.

Smith, Linda Wasmer. *Louis Pasteur: Disease Fighter*. Berkeley Heights, NJ: Enslow Publishers, 1997.
Smith has created a stirring portrait of the scientist, which is enhanced by historic photographs and drawings.

Stalking the Mysterious Microbe!
http://www.microbe.org/
The American Society for Microbiology has created an award-winning site packed with facts, photographs, news, movies, and interviews.

Swertka, Eve, and Albert Swertka. *A Chilling Story: How Things Cool Down*. Englewood Cliffs, NJ: Julian Messner, 1991.
Practical experiments reinforce skillful explanations of the science of refrigeration.

Ventura, Piero. *Food: Its Evolution through the Ages*. Boston: Houghton Mifflin Company, 1994.
Illustrations enhance a thorough overview of the history of planting, harvesting, and preserving food.

Whitman, Sylvia. *What's Cooking? The History of American Food*. Minneapolis: Lerner Publications Company, 2001.
In entertaining fashion, Whitman traces America's eating habits from the "four Bs"—bacon, beans, butter, and bread to modern health foods such as prune sauce pizza.

Chapter Opener Photo Captions

About the Author

Years of travel to natural and historic places inspire and inform the work of author and photographer Judith Jango-Cohen. Her thirty-four children's books reflect the depth of these experiences. Her books have been listed in Best Books for Children, recommended by the National Science Teacher's Association, and chosen for the Children's Literature Choice List.

Photo Acknowledgments

The images in this book are used with the permission of: © Underwood Photo Archives/SuperStock, pp. 4–5; © Bettmann/CORBIS, pp. 6, 9, 14, 28; Minnesota Historical Society, p. 12; Library of Congress, pp. 15 (LC-D4-24857), 29 (LC-USE6-008766), 34 (LC-USZ62-94680); © CORBIS, pp. 17, 21; © Charles O'Rear/CORBIS, p. 20; Chicago Historical Society, p. 24; © H. Armstrong Roberts/CORBIS, p. 27; Immigrant City Archives, Inc., p. 31; © Brown Brothers, p. 32; © Najlah Feanny/CORBIS SABA, p. 37; Agricultural Research Service, USDA, p. 38; © Ed Young/CORBIS, p. 41; © LWA-Stephen Welstead/CORBIS, p. 42; © Mark E. Gibson/CORBIS, pp. 46–47. Cover photos: top, courtesy of Harry Lerner; bottom, © Rick Friedman/CORBIS. Montgomery Ward & Co.: back cover, p. 1, all borders